Conservation of Tropical Fruit Tree Genetic Resources with Focus on Utilization

ATPBR
Breeding for Prosperity

ADVANCED TRAINING IN PLANT BREEDING (ATPBR)

A15, Amrut Sai Sara City, Nakshtrawadi, Paithan Road, Aurangabad, Maharashtra-431001

nipa®

NIPA® GENX ELECTRONIC RESOURCES & SOLUTIONS P. LTD.

New Delhi-110 034

Dr. Aparna Tiwari
Co-Founder, Director – ATPBR

Aparna Tiwari is Co-founder and Chief Executive Officer at the Foundation for Advanced Training in Plant breeding (ATPBR), where she leads professional training, technology liaising, awareness sessions, and other capacity building activities. She has worked previously in various positions with the FAO (Food and Agriculture Organization), Monsanto India Pvt. Ltd., ICRISAT (International Crops Research Institute for the Semi-Arid Tropics), and the MGM– Institute of Technology. She obtained her MSc and PhD from the Wageningen University, The Netherlands, and her Bachelor's (BSc) from Banaras Hindu University sity. She has authored two books and published several research papers in peer-reviewed international journals and conferences.

About ATPBR

ATPBR is a registered not-for-profit Foundation, based in India, which works in close collaboration with Seed Industry, Institutions, NGOs, and Government bodies, to impart training in plant breeding to develop future-ready plant breeders. It is India's leading networking training organization, with full-fledged expertise and resources for capacity building, market linkages, policy advocacy, and project management. Main objective of ATPBR is to develop a sustainable and thriving agricultural system to serve farmers, support emerging entrepreneurs and assist industries to build market-driven competencies in Human Resources. ATPBR is open to collaborate with diverse range of organizations, academic and research institutions, NGOs, independent professionals and aspire to meet the intellectual needs to make crop improvement an attractive and lucrative domain for all concerned.

Dr. V. Ramanatha Rao
Former Senior Scientist, Bioversity International
and Co-Founder, GRSV Consulting Services

Speaker

Dr. V. Ramanatha Rao is an undergraduate from Tirupathi and a postgraduate from APAU, Rajendranagar in agricultural sciences, and did his doctorate in Genetics from IARI, New Delhi in 1975. After briefly working at the All India Coordinated Rice Improvement Project, Rajendranagar, he joined the International Crops Research Institute for the Semi Arid Tropics (ICRISAT), Hyderabad to work on the genetic resources of groundnut. In between, he worked on sabbatical leave at CENARGEN, Brasilia, Brazil to establish Arachis genetic resources collection. While at ICRISAT, he helped in establishing the groundnut germplasm world collection including several wild relatives. He joined IBPGR (International Beaureau of Plant Genetic Resources) (which later became IPGRI (International Plant Genetic Resources Institute), and then Bioversity International). He worked at its offices in Rome, Italy (1989-'92); Singapore (1992-'96) and Kuala Lumpur, Malaysia (1997-2007). His work ranged widely and covered various aspects of plant genetic resources conservation and use – of both crop and forestry species and covered many PGR disciplines- genetic diversity studies, utilization of germplasm, ex situ, in situ and complementary conservation strategies, and policies and programmes, PGR networks and collaboration, science and application, leadership and teamwork, the balance between IPGRI's objectives and partners' needs; at various levels of the organisation- national, subregional, regional, and global levels. He helped several countries in Asia to establish and/or develop national plant genetic resources programmes. He was Honorary Research Fellow with Bioversity International from 2008 to 2014. During the little over 30 years of involvement in PGR work, he has published, over 300 papers/reports/chapters and books. Currently, he is the Co-Founder of GRSV Consulting Services. His main work, with the help of other co-founders and the Chief Editor, was to develop the monthly AgriTech Newsletter.

Dr. M. J. Vasudeva Rao
Adviser: Training, ATPBR
and Co-Founder, GRSV Consulting Services, Bangalore

Moderator

Dr. M. J. Vasudeva Rao, has clocked one and a half decades of plant breeding-related work experience in UAS-Bangalore, ICAR, ICRISAT and, later, for close to three decades in multinational seed companies in India in a range of responsibilities from Breeding to Research Management to Business management. He started his professional plant breeding career as an ARS Scientist (ICAR) at AICRIPDA and AICSIP Hyderabad. Moved to ICRISAT, Hyderabad as a Plant Breeder in Sorghum with a focus on Striga resistance. He worked in various capacities in Advanta India (earlier names ICI Seeds, ITC Zeneca) and finally held the position of Sr. Vice President. He was President of Agricultural Technology at Metahelix Life Sciences Limited a TATA group company. He has made significant contributions to the development of several varieties and hybrids, new selection technologies, and mentoring NextGen performing plant breeders. He has published many books, book chapters, and over 100 research papers, conference presentations, invited talks, etc., on seeds, plant breeding-related areas, IPR, and Biotechnology.

Conservation of Tropical Fruit Tree Genetic Resources with Focus on Utilization

WebCon Series 18

V. Ramanatha Rao
Former Senior Scientist
Bioversity International
and Co-Founder, GRSV Consulting Services

ATPBR
Breeding for Prosperity

ADVANCED TRAINING IN PLANT BREEDING (ATPBR)
A15, Amrut Sai Sara City, Nakshtrawadi, Paithan Road, Aurangabad, Maharashtra-431001

nipa®

NIPA® GENX ELECTRONIC RESOURCES & SOLUTIONS P. LTD.
New Delhi-110 034

ADVANCED TRAINING IN PLANT BREEDING (ATPBR)

NIPA® GENX ELECTRONIC RESOURCES & SOLUTIONS P. LTD.

101,103, Vikas Surya Plaza, CU Block
L.S.C.Market, Pitam Pura, New Delhi-110 034
Ph : +91 11 27341616, 27341717, 27341718
E-mail: newindiapublishingagency@gmail.com
Website: www. nipabooks.com

For customer assistance, please contact
Phone: + 91-11-27 34 17 17
Fax: + 91-11-27 34 16 16
E-Mail: feedbacks@nipabooks.com

ISBN: 978-93-58874-16-7

Published and Exclusively Distributed by NIPA

"This WebCon is compiled and transcribed by Dr. M.J. Vasudeva Rao, currently a member of the Training Advisory Board of ATPBR"

Edited by Aruna T Kumar

Composed and Designed by NIPA®.

Preface

ATPBR is bringing eminent plant breeders who have achieved laurels in not just science of plant breeding, but have excelled in other related areas like policy, administration, etc., to meet practicing and potential plant breeders on a platform called ATPBR Webinar series regularly every month. These Web-based Conferences (WebCon) have been hugely successful as seen by the numbers of participants from India and outside of India. The WebCon series captures the presentations in a published format which includes key messages delivered by the speakers.

Contents

Conservation of Tropical Fruit Tree Genetic Resources with a Focus on Utilization

Dr. V. Ramanatha Rao

At the outset, I need to state that I am not a horticultural specialist and whatever horticulture knowledge have, is gained on the job and I am a plant genetic resources specialist with an interest in biodiversity and have worked across Asia. Today we will be mainly talking about tropical fruits and, in particular, tropical fruit tree genetic resources. If you look at tree fruits as a group, it includes a large number of species, unlike in field crops, e.g., rice, wheat, maize, etc., where just a few species are involved in each crop. Here we are talking about a group of species under each fruit tree. While talking about them, certain generalizations have to be made. Also, there are many unexploited species which are waiting to be discovered for human usage and exploitation, and there is hardly any genetic information available about them. There is a huge gap in this respect, and whether anytime anyone will be working on them is also not certain at this point.

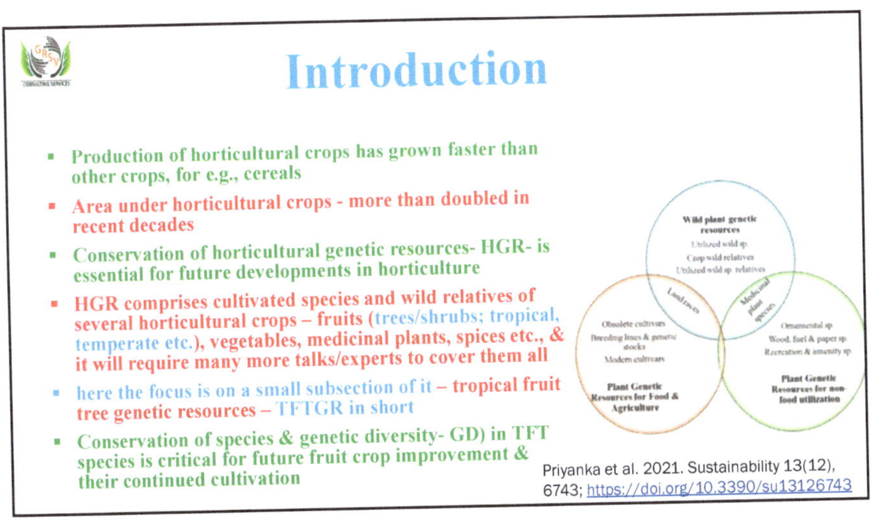

Today's topic is about tree genetic resources of tropical fruits. As an introduction, I would like to point out that horticultural crop production has been growing faster than field crops production, and hence the genetic resources of tropical fruits especially trees are also increasing tremendously. There have been many ongoing efforts of conserving many of these horticultural species and different institutions world over are involved. However, there are several drawbacks to them which we will touch upon as we go along. Horticultural genetic resources comprise cultivated species and wild relatives of several horticultural crops like fruits, vegetables, medical plants, spices, etc. and they include trees, shrubs, both tropical and temperate. Each of them is having its own requirements for conservation. Therefore, covering this large topic will require many sessions. Hence, today we will focus on a small subsection of this topic which is tropical fruit tree genetic diversity - conservation and utilisation.

In the world, plant genetic resources and wildlife collection and conservation efforts have been going on for a long time.

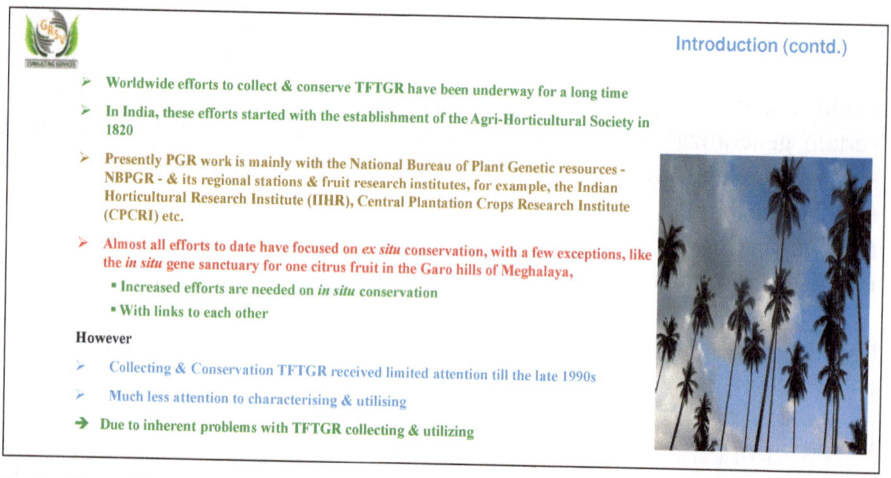

In India, efforts to collect, conserve and utilize tropical fruit tree genetic diversity started way back in 1820 during the British Raj under the aegis of the Agri-Horticultural Society. Presently most of the work on horticultural genetic resources conservation is carried out under the guidance of the National Bureau of Plant Genetic Resources and various Horticultural Regional Research Institutes. For example, we have the Indian Institute of Horticultural Research and Central Plantation Crops Research Institute and other institutions where conservation and utilization work related to their mandated crops is undertaken. One important thing to note is that almost all our efforts to date have focused on *ex situ* conservation. There are but a few exceptions like the establishment of *in situ* gene sanctuary in citrus, mainly for one species only (*Citrus indica*) in Garo Hills of Meghalaya. Although it was established long ago, not many people have shown interest in going there and studying those species. We need increased efforts in conserving *in situ* because many of the tree species, wild forms and their wild relatives occur in forest areas. This is very important in the case of fruit tree species collection and conservation.

Although collecting tropical fruit trees started only in 1990 in India, researchers and others have been collecting them even before in other countries. However, the concept of collecting genetic diversity came into the picture more recently. For example in India, it was mainly collecting what has been referred to as 'elite' trees – trees which produced the most desirable fruits and appeared to have high yields. In most tree species, collecting genetic diversity as done in the case of rice or wheat or other cereal crops or legumes, where population samples are collected, was not in vogue. Only in 1990, we tried to change this a little bit. Even today it is not practised everywhere but relative to before the 1990s, we are in a much better situation. This was/is mainly due to genetic diversity sampling issues in tree species, the land area needed to plant a representative accession, and selecting useful accessions takes long-term characterization and evaluation.

Given the nature of the fruit trees like perenniality, long gestation period, and large extent of land that is required to conserve them *ex situ*, characterization and utilization have received much less attention. For example, one can evaluate thousands of groundnut varieties in an acre of land. One cannot do the same thing with mangoes - one species of mango, *Mangifera indica*, alone has over 700 different varieties, and even planting just one tree would take about 7ha planning (100-110 trees per hectare for a full expression of tree traits, we cannot practice high-density planting etc., as the accessions need characterization). In addition to *M. indica,* there are other mango species which are consumed in Southeast Asian countries. In that sense, the evaluation outcome relative to other annual crop species, is much less due to the inherent problems with tree species. These are similar problems in other forest tree species because of which collection and utilization efforts in managing genetic diversity have been pretty slow. However, as one realized the importance of having a considerable amount of genetic diversity in tree species for present and future use, especially given the emergence of harsh climatic conditions that are emerging, more efforts to collect genetic diversity in tree species are being given increased attention.

Introduction (contd.)

Challenges in better conservation & use of TFTGR

- Focus on collecting elite material, poor representation of wild relatives
- Inadequate sample size
- Methods of collecting & transfer to genebank, etc.
- Availability of space and methods for conservation
- Limited GD conserved
- Poor characterization, evaluation & documentation
- Long gestation period
- Modern methods - marker-assisted, genetic transformation, gene-editing
  - Some progress was reported in grapes, citrus, apple, papaya etc., most TFT species yet to be developed
  - See Hortic Res 2021 8:166. https://doi.org/10.1038/s41438-021-00601-3 & Bioengineering 2022, 9:176. https://doi.org/10.3390/bioengineering9040176

Hence

- Conservation of a larger pool of species & GD of TFT
- Characterize & evaluation
- Genetic enhancement & access
- Better & faster crop improvement methods

The basics of collection and conservation include collecting by going out into the fields or forests, collecting new samples of different plant species and bringing them back to conserve them either in seed banks, field genebanks, in *in vitro* collections, or as freeze-dried samples stored at around -196^{0}Cusing liquid nitrogen. These are various methods that are used for collections, details of which may be found in any basic plant genetic resources textbooks. As noted earlier, most of the time, the germplasm collectors collect only a small number of elite materials (with immediate use in mind) from a large population of the species, which doesn't represent the genetic diversity of that species. It does not also serve the purpose of characterizing and evaluating genetic diversity in the species. However, users of such incomplete collections have done significant work even with that limited collections and it would be better to collect more seeds/propagules per population during collection expeditions. There are also problems with methods of collection and transfer to the genebank, especially with fruit tree species most of which are recalcitrant, i.e., one cannot collect and dry the seeds as they lose viability rapidly. Only a few tropical fruits, such as papaya, bananas, guava and chiku, and most others produce recalcitrant seeds. Recalcitrant seeds only germinate as long as the seed moisture content is above 14% while some of them require up to 22% moisture to be viable. Cereals and other legumes have orthodox seeds as they can be dried to very low moisture content and stored in cold conditions. Also, the size of the seeds/fruits in some fruit trees can be large, e.g., jackfruit, which can be a problem for collecting. For some fruit tree species, *in vitro* collecting techniques are available, but for many others, appropriate methods are yet to be developed and standardized. However, for many of the underutilized species, there are no protocols available yet. So, it is difficult to develop high-quality collections. These are some of the technical challenges that need to be resolved.

Other challenges in the case of fruit tree germplasm are the prohibitive land and other infrastructure support required to establish and manage the collections. For example, for a crop species like mango, to conserve 100 accessions of 40 trees for each accession (roughly, collecting seed or propagules 40 individual trees being a minimum number of a sample size to capture alleles with a probability of about 90%), huge pockets of land will be required. And managing these large collections would require appropriate financial and technical personnel. However, appropriate budget and infrastructure need to be provided in larger and longer-term interests of conserving them for future generations. Often, because of these challenges, the limited genetic diversity of many of the fruit species has been conserved.

Because of such limitations, characterization and evaluation work have also not been completed in many cases. A lot more needs to be done in the area of characterization, evaluation and documentation. Good examples are available for some of the major fruit species which can be used for other fruit species as well. Another challenge is the long gestation period in the fruit trees. It takes a long time from planting to flowering to the production of seeds or getting good clonal material out of it. Even if one can obtain clonal material early on for propagation, one needs to wait for fruit and seed production for evaluating productivity and quality traits. So, collecting, characterizing, evaluating and using fruit tree genetic resources requires a different approach than the one used for annual species.

Some of the modern methods like marker-assisted selection, genetic transformation, re-generation, etc., have been available for some species like grapes, citrus, apple, papaya and some vegetable species. Actually, in the case of tomatoes, some of these methods have been used in the last two decades. These methods are not generally available for hard-wooded species, tropical species like mango, etc., because tissue culture protocols are not available. However, scientists are trying to overcome these problems and some good research articles are available now which may be referred to. For example, recently there was a study providing details of regeneration protocols for longan, *Dimocarpus longan,* a tropical fruit tree species from Southeast Asia. The fruit is very well-liked and is very nutritious. Some growers have tried to grow longan in Kerala and the high rainfall zones but have not been very successful to date. Because of these challenges, the conservation of a larger pool of species and genetic diversity of tropical fruits is not achieved and requires much more effort in terms of human resources as well as financial resources. Similar is the case for their characterization and evaluation. As I mentioned earlier, standardized methods, for collecting, characterization and evaluation are not yet available for several of the minor under-utilized fruit tree species Some scientists have been working with these under-utilized fruit tree species, but in a limited capacity and with limited resources.

Regarding genetic enhancement and access to fruit tree genetic resources, most of them, especially the wild ones, require a certain amount of pre-breeding efforts before the breeders can make use of the germplasm. This could be done by germplasm curators themselves or jointly with crop improvement research. Genetically enhancement improves the utilisation of conserved material by breeders. Breeders are already overloaded with doing what they have to do and if the pre-breeding efforts are also put on their shoulders, it will be tough for them. The enhanced material cannot just stay in the genebanks, just as items in a museum, they need to be used for crop improvement. In addition, such efforts give further visibility to germplasm managers, and not be considered just as a service and make their work more interesting and productive. However, one must be careful not to do such work at the cost of germplasm management.

In addition to germplasm enhancement or pre-breeding efforts, we also need better and faster crop improvement methods because of the long gestation period in tropical fruit crops. It is almost prohibitive to do large-scale crossing and testing before releasing any varieties for large-scale cultivation. Often the varieties are released without much testing and that could be one reason why many of the tropical fruit tree varieties have failed. So modern methods of plant breeding, like speed breeding methods, can help in better using genetic resources.

These are some of the examples of species that we are concerned about here like mango, jackfruit, mangosteen, avocado, etc. There are more than 25-30 important tropical fruits in India and not all of them are trees. Southeast Asia and the Americas have a large number of such tree fruits. South America, for example, has 400 usable tropical fruit tree species apart from non-tree fruits such as Passiflora, etc.

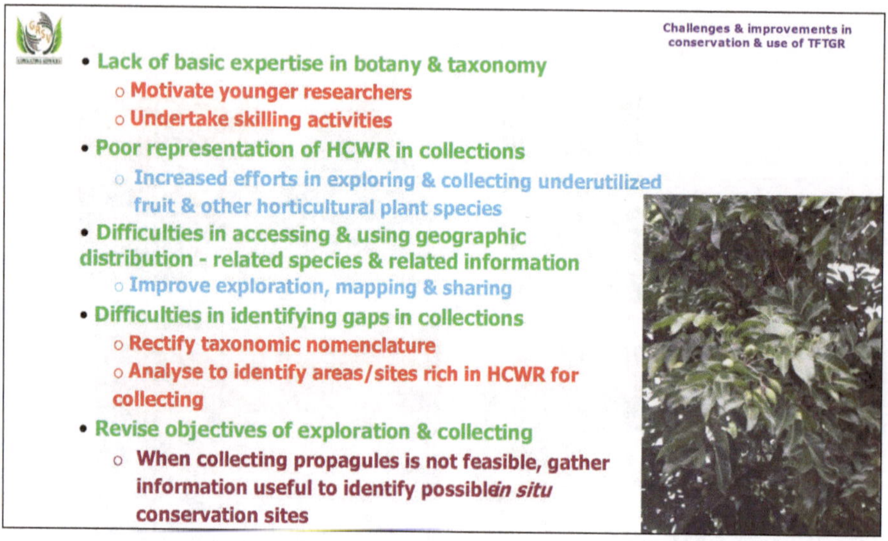

Let us continue and see if we can provide answers to the challenges mentioned earlier. One of the challenges is the lack of basic expertise in botany and taxonomy among genetic diversity managers. The only way to overcome this challenge, especially in India, is to improve biology education and improve the interest students take in acquiring knowledge and developing skills in plant taxonomy and descriptive botany. The next challenge is the poor representation of wild relatives in many horticultural collections. E.g., there are over 700 to 1000 varieties of mango, however, India does not have many wild relatives in its mango collections, except *Mangifera andamanica*, *M. sylvatica* (some consider it as just a wild form of *M. indica*), and the occasional reference to *M. odorata*. But even the numbers of these species represented in the collections are very few. In Southeast Asia, where all the other relatives of mango occur, some of which are consumed if not cultivated. In their collections or even in their distribution maps, the basic information on accession species identification is minimal. For example, most of the areas where many *Mangifera* species occur and have been collected are identified as only *Mangifera* spp. as the collectors and staff at the genebank lack the requisite taxonomic knowledge to identify the species correctly. However, collections even though identified only to the genus level, are good and deserve conservation. In many regions, even single trees occurring in the wild have been protected by local people. We understand their difficulties in accessing and using geographic information and promote expertise in taxonomy and ecogeographic distribution, where possible. The newer versions of GPS and GIS systems are helping greatly in this matter in identifying the location of collections, but if one does not have taxonomic information about the accession, it is incomplete. In many species, a lack of taxonomic information limits its effective conservation and utilisation.

Regarding the challenge of gaps in collections, I am sure that even in major established cereal and legume collections, there are several gaps. To identify gaps in the collections, we must have passport data and the geographic coordinates of collection sites, along with taxonomic information. In the absence of such information, it is almost impossible to identify geographic gaps in collections. If we have full characterization and evaluation information, we can identify gaps in the genetic diversity in a collection and then look for the missing genetic diversity or even make a collection expedition for adding the missing traits in a collection through targeted collecting.

In most exploration missions, the objectives of the collection mission are set at the beginning. Some of the funding agencies are strict about achieving the pre-set objectives and allow very few deviations. However, we have seen over the years that many times the objectives need to be revised or modified as one goes along with the mission. Due to the poor information before the start of the expedition, one might visit areas where either flowering and fruiting are over or yet to start. In such cases, one can only collect information about the occurrence of trees, about any communities that are utilizing or involved in managing and seek their help later in collection missions.

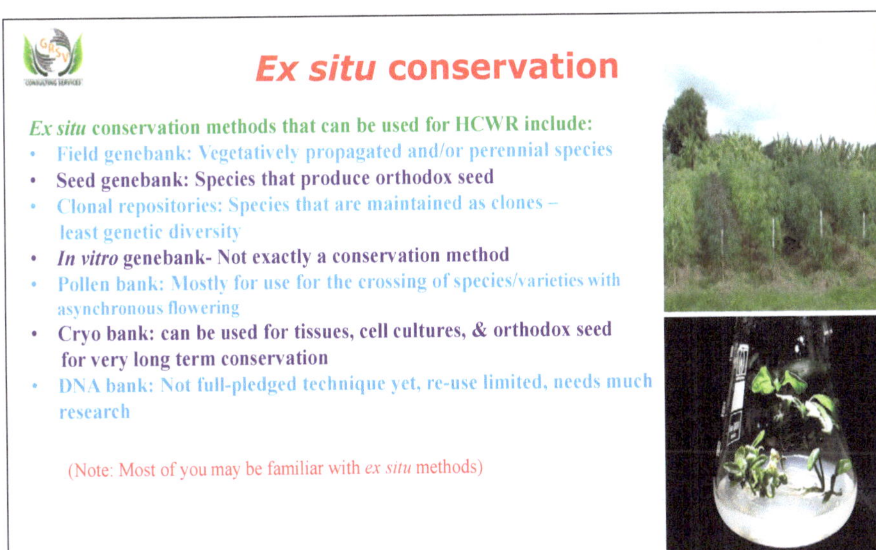

Ex situ conservation is where the germplasm is conserved outside its natural habitat or genebanks in research institutions, botanical gardens, etc. There are detailed guidelines for the establishment and management of *ex situ* collections by the FAO, Bioversity International and other organizations are available. Conserving seeds is much easier, but many fruit tree species with recalcitrant seeds need to be conserved in field genebanks. In most other cases, the method of conservation used could be cryobanks or even DNA banks. Pollen banks may primarily use for conserving pollen to tide over the seasonal imbalances that may occur because of the different flowering periods of different species or different accessions. As mentioned earlier there are many technical guides as well as publications that you can refer to.

In situ Conservation

TFTGR – being perennial species are candidates for conservation *in situ*

Challenges & Needs

Little has been done to date
- Enhance actions & policy support
- improve research & training

Close involvement of growers & communities
- Internalize conservation actions with growers & forest dwellers' activities
- Train PGR staff in Participatory Methods to work with communities

Understanding concerns of the people dependent on NTFPs
- Understand local needs & local uses
- Avoid top-down-approach

***In situ* conservation is not feasible in all situations**
- *In situ* conservation is context-specific
- Integrate conservation of TFTGR conservation with PAs, reserves etc.
- Develop/modify forest management plans to include TFTGR

Limited allocation of resources- financial & human
- Demonstrate the feasibility & Importance
- Generate funds & approvals for optimal level of staffing

We now come to *in situ* conservation, which I think is important for conserving tropical fruit tree germplasm because of their size, long gestation period, and the funds required to manage them well in *ex situ* collection. *In situ* conservation is one of two basic conservation strategies, along with *ex situ* conservation. Article 8 of the Convention on Biological Diversity (CBD) specifies *in situ* conservation as the primary conservation strategy and states that *ex situ* measures should play a supportive role (serve as a backup) to reach conservation targets. *In situ* conservation aims to enable biodiversity to maintain itself within the context of the ecosystem in which it is found. Traditionally, protected areas have been seen as the cornerstone of in-situ conservation. Very little has been done to overcome many hurdles in upscaling *in situ* conservation. For example, as noted earlier, we have a citrus sanctuary in Meghalaya, but for that, there are hardly any examples of *in situ* conservation even outside India. There are some community-managed sites in Southeast Asia and South America, and a few exist in India, especially in the western ghats in Tamil Nadu. There is no organized effort in *in situ* conservation.

It should be strongly emphasized that unless conservation becomes a priority and institutionalised, it is going to be very difficult to sustain it for a long time. We need to enhance policy support as well as research and training. I believe increased support for promoting *in situ* conservation, especially for training, should be a priority for the national plant genetic resources programme. There is a need for close involvement with the growers and communities. Though this is well known that communities need to be involved in conservation when it comes to implementation, it's almost always a top-down approach which hinders the entire process, and nothing works out later. This is very much linked to the need to understand the concerns of the people who are dependent on the material being targeted for conservation. I am not advocating conservation at the cost of people's livelihoods, but their needs must be integrated in any conservation effort with the farmers and communities being the primary stockholders. A few examples are available in our country where the forest dwellers and tribals have been evacuated from locations for saving certain animals and plant species which is a very poor approach to the whole process. Because of this, the whole thing melts down very fast, and at the end of the day, nothing will be left. Hence, one must avoid a top-down approach. More recently, there have been cases where greater emphasis was placed on community involvement in managing genetic resources. Even if the locals need to be taught some modern concepts, it is better to approach them as if the locals know about them and they own them. In many cases, researchers have learnt from the locals (traditional knowledge). *In situ* conservation is not feasible in all situations and it is context specific. It is possible only in some areas and some contexts. In addition, the conservation efforts must be beneficial to the local communities for the success of any such effort. So, we have to identify that context and only carry it out in that area with those communities and for those species. The most common challenge is the limited allocation of financial resources, which needs to be remedied if indeed biodiversity in tropical fruits species, and general conservation of any biodiversity, has to succeed.

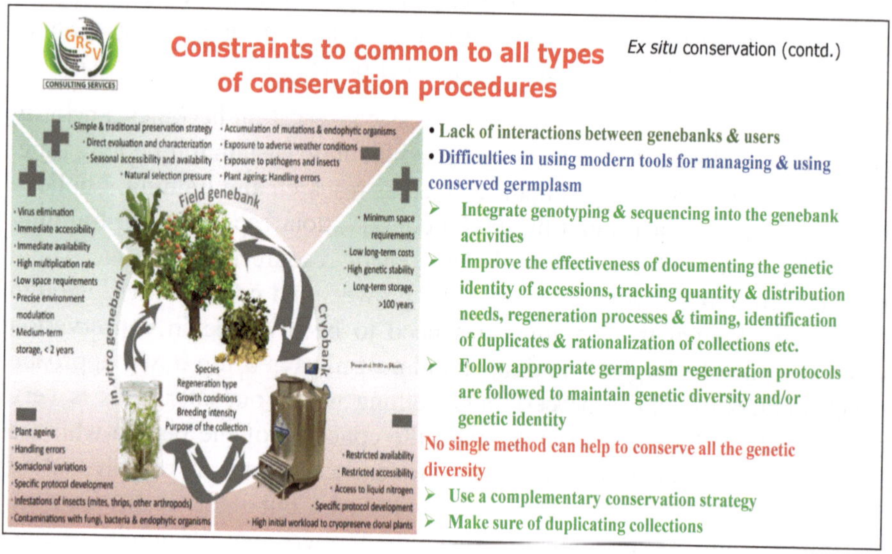

Let us now consider the constraints to all types of conservation, including both *in situ* and *ex situ* conservations which are currently available. Each level of conservation is linked to each other from collecting to field genebanks to *in vitro* genebanks to cryogenic banks, etc., These links provide information on different actions that need to be carried out while managing or while setting up the protocols to manage the collections. One thing that we will find in any conservation effort is the lack of interaction between genebank managers and the users of these banks. Each group carries out what it does best without any interactions. This is a major hurdle to achieve efficiency from characterization and evaluation to its ultimate utilisation and needs to be overcome.

There are difficulties in using modern tools, especially in the case of tropical fruit crop germplasm, several of these tools are difficult to deal with. All modern methods of conservation when made available, especially regeneration methods in hard woody perennials like mango, etc., will be tough to deal with. We can conclude that no single method is useful for conserving most of the genetic diversity that we require for the future, especially considering what is likely to emerge due to climate change factors. We have to evolve a better strategy that we have been naming as 'systems approach' that will take care of, almost in entirety, all actions required, all human resources required, using the available finances which will deal with this situation well. This approach will be dynamic, contributing to newer developments of managing and incorporating new technologies as the become available, without forgetting about integrating local/traditional/indigenous knowledge.

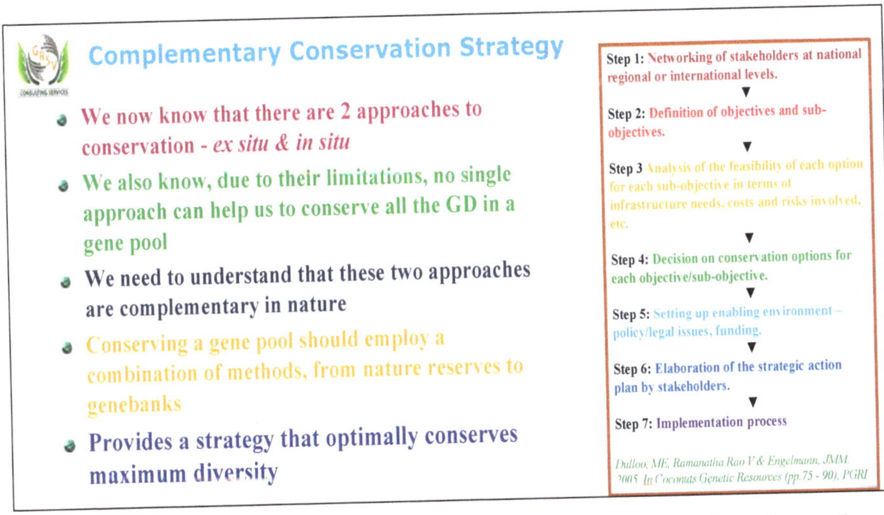

This is what we call a complementary conservation strategy. There is no clear-cut hard and fast division between *ex situ* and *in situ* conservation approaches– it is a spectrum of conservation efforts, often with no clear-cut boundaries and is executed in totality. The information on the right provides some guidelines on how to go from one level to the next level. In any case, one should know the networking of all stakeholders at national and international levels, define the objectives and analyse the feasibilities of each option then make the decisions regarding conservation options. Setting up the enabling environment at the policy, legal and funding levels, and elaborating the strategy for the consequent action by all stakeholders has to be carried out. This was explained by us and others in 2005. However, even today we find it difficult to find good examples of such efforts and there are major gaps between actually what is being done and something that should be done.

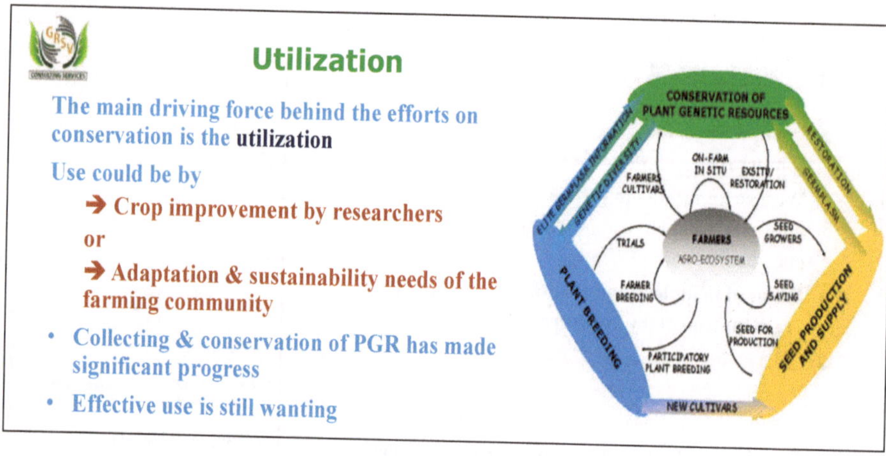

Coming to the utilization part, I will touch upon just a few of the things. In case of tropical fruit trees, utilization of the germplasm is a tough job because of the inherent issues that are specific to this group of species. The picture in the slide which is from FAO, provides some guidelines on how conservation, plant breeding, seed production and supply are interlinked. These can be further linked to different processes and to the farmers or ecosystems in which they are grown. I think this is a simple concept and most of you will be able to access this information easily. You can write to me if you have any issues regarding plant genetic resources of not just tropical fruits but also any other group of crops. You can email to me at (vramanatharao@gmail.com). At GRSV what we do is to share the knowledge. So, we will try and share as much as possible.

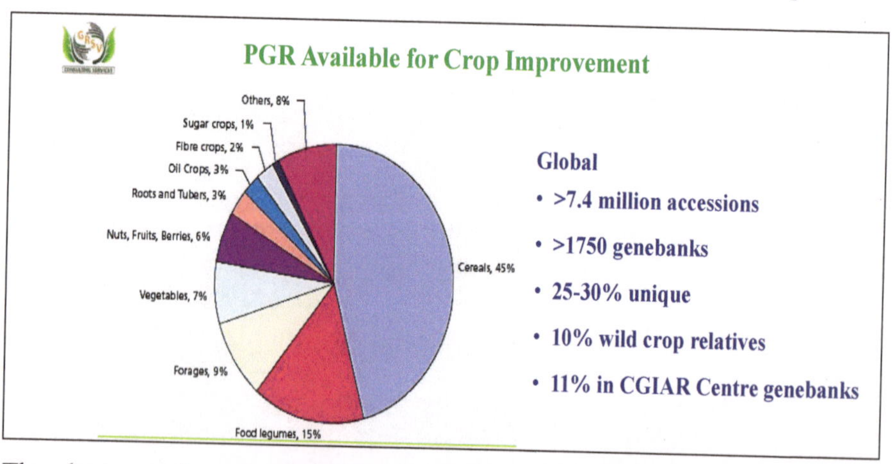

The plant genetic resources that are available for crop improvement are over 7.4 million accessions conserved in 1750 genebanks around the globe. About

25-30% may be unique and the rest are duplicates. Duplicates in genetic resources are not considered a waste. It is a good safety backup. A certain amount of duplication becomes essential because the breeders in different countries are working on similar problems and they have to have access to similar germplasm. Out of the 7.4 million accessions, about 10% are wild crop relatives. About 11% are in CGIAR centre genebanks. You can see in the pie chart that cereals and food legumes make up the bulk of germplasm conserved. Roots and tubers, some horticultural crops, fruit and nuts, berries and vegetables make up the rest. Some of the oilseed crops are also represented. However, plantation crops and spices are missing here, and so are the medicinal plants.

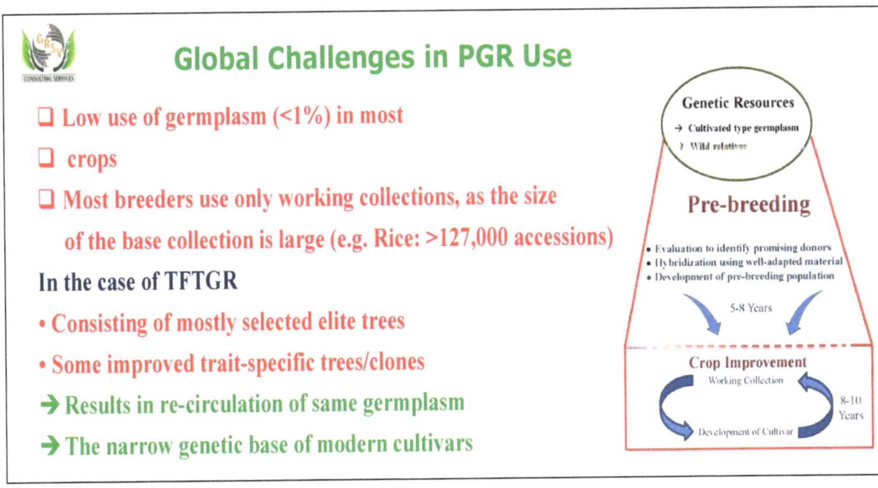

Earlier we have seen local challenges for effective use of conserved plant genetic resources. Let us look at the global challenges for the utilization of plant genetic resources. At the global level, germplasm utilization is low and they are hardly used. We have always been talking about the importance of germplasm and how useful it can be for the future and the present. However, only less than one per cent of germplasm in most crops is used, with some exceptions in wheat and maize. With the invention of modern tools of plant breeding, even in these crops, it is coming down. When molecular biology came into being, molecular biologists told us that we don't require any germplasm and we can pick up the genes from, for example, a banana from the market and get hold of the requisite gene. But I think that was too optimistic and things have been proven to be different. Phenotype remains an important consideration. Most breeders use only working collections with them, which they maintain regularly. After 1992, it has become difficult to get germplasm from another country. Many institutions do not have the wherewithal, i.e.

resources, land or finances, to establish and manage their collections. In the case of tropical fruit tree germplasm, there are additional problems which we have already gone through earlier.

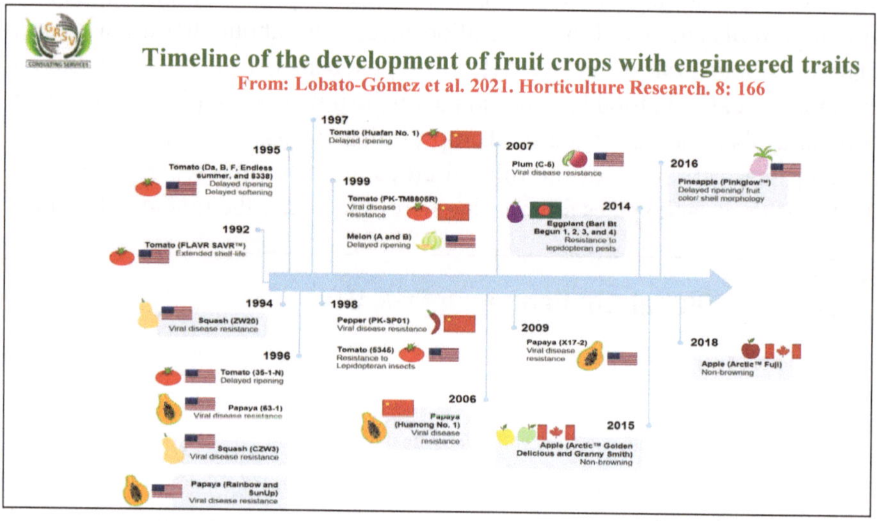

Even for simple crop improvement starting with germplasm, following the timeline in the chart, it will take eight to ten years and one may add few more years if one is dealing with tropical fruit trees. With the use of modern methods like genetic engineering, gene editing, CRISPR, marker-assisted breeding, etc., the pictures shown here will change a little bit in terms of the amount of time it takes to develop an improved crop variety starting from germplasm. (I have used this slide especially because it talks mostly about fruits). As I mentioned earlier, the work on some of the fruits like tomatoes, papaya, and squash, started a decade or two ago, and some products of that work are available in the market now. For further progress to be made using these modern tools and technologies, especially in tropical fruits, regeneration protocols need to be perfected. Researchers are trying to bypass even the need for regeneration but still on a small scale and in a few laboratories. So this gives you some idea of how things are progressing from way back in 1992 to now. But at the end of the day, with the challenges of global warming, climate change, erratic rainfalls, etc., we have set ourselves the task of making agricultural production, including tropical fruits, a sustainable and climate-resilient one.

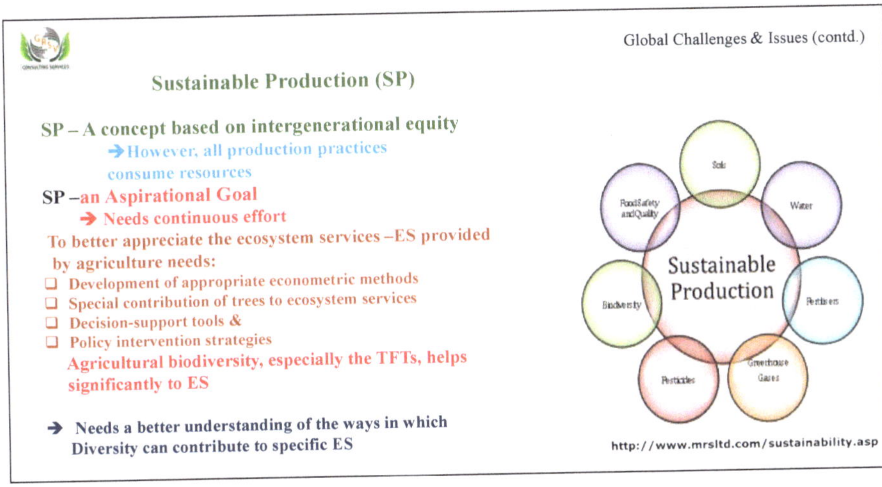

Now sustainability is the buzzword. Sustainability means that any system must sustain itself over time. Sustainable production is essential and this sustainable production is not in just agriculture but in everything else we do. But let's confine to agriculture here. The concept of sustainability is based on intergenerational equity. Sustainable food production is in growing crops in sustainable ways to meet society's present food needs, without compromising the ability of current or future generations to meet their needs. It can be based on an understanding of ecosystem services. Practitioners of sustainable food production seek to integrate three main objectives into their work: a healthy environment, economic profitability, and social and economic equity. It is something to do with equality and justice for all. However, all production practices consume a certain level of resources. So, the key question is how well we can manage these resources and how well we manage the waste products coming out of that and continue to do sustainable production. This aspirational goal cannot be achieved easily. However, there is no option for us other than working continuously towards this aspirational goal. We need to better appreciate ecosystem services which are provided for agriculture. Some of those services are soils, water, fertilizers or nutrition, greenhouse gases that are emitted and how to reduce them or how to use them, pesticides and how to get rid of them as much as possible, and biodiversity and its conservation. All these without expanding the land which has been blamed and rightly so for the increased agricultural production and food safety and quality. If food is safe for a longer period and the quality is maintained for a longer period there will be less and less wastage. Globally about 14 to 18 % of the food is wasted making it imperative for us to produce additional food. Not just that, the wastage adds to pollution because much of it is not composted or to reused in any way. These are some of the challenges and continuous efforts are needed for achieving this objective.

The current economic parameters available for measuring the growth, production and development of a country need to be revised drastically. We recently published a blog about GDP and the conclusion was that it is not going to help. It has to be based on the human development index. We also need decision support tools, for example, to help make soils healthier. Some of the aspects we need to be looking at in the future are how to improve soil health, how we use water economically and with little wastage, and how to make plants more efficient producers and resilient to changing climate. Agricultural biodiversity especially in tropical fruit trees helps significantly in providing ecosystem services. If you compare the fruit tree species with herbaceous species, you will observe that they have the additional advantages of the ability to recycle water and gases and provide many other ecosystem services, along with nutritious food. This can be achieved by appropriate planting and management of diverse tropical fruit species. So, besides food production, they play a major role in improving our ecosystem health.

Opportunities for Improvement Using PGR

Demands placed by climate change

Agriculture is a victim of climate change as well it is the means for mitigating

AGBDY -the biological basis of innovation & resilience

Proper ecosystem management & biodiversity provides several ecosystem services

➔ Resilient, productive, & sustainable systems, including

- ❑ **Control of pests & disease**
- ❑ **Regulation of microclimate**
- ❑ **Decomposition of wastes**
- ❑ **Regulation of nutrient cycles, &**
- ❑ **Crop pollination, etc.**

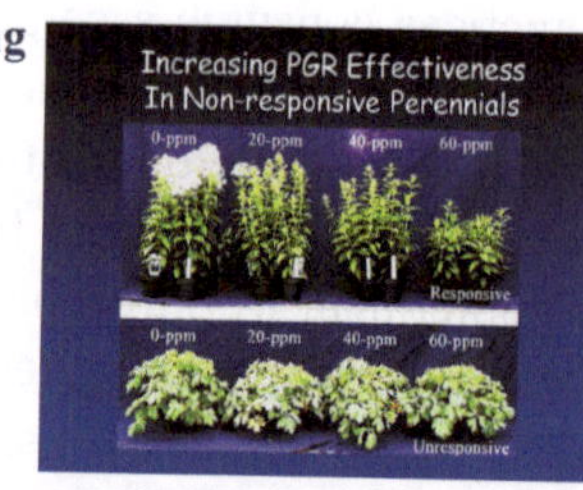

So let us now look at improving the use of plant genetic resources. We have noted earlier that less than one per cent or so of plant genetic resources is used in research and crop improvement. But as the literature tells us, in the last few years especially starting from 2015 or so, agriculture is both a victim as well as a mitigating tool for adverse impacts of climate change. It is a victim of climate change especially if you remove animals from the equation, agricultural production has much less impact on climate. However, they contribute considerably to pollution through the use of pesticides and fertilizers, which also increase the cost of production. People are always looking for increasing productivity per unit area by using more inputs. This thinking requires change as this type of production system is not sustainable. Agricultural biodiversity, the biological basis of innovation and resilience, can provide some solutions in this direction. I indicated this while dealing with the characterization and evaluation of biodiversity. The major food crops, let us say the top ten crops, need to be improved for the traits that we will be looking for breeding in the next 10 to 15 years so that the temperatures don't go beyond 1.5°C, or the desert doesn't expand, and our water sources are not polluted leading to deterioration in soil health because of the extensive use of chemicals. Some traits can be found in the genetic resources that are available either in *ex situ* collections or in the wild areas. If we can use this agricultural biodiversity we can become more resilient and productive and create sustainable systems in the future. This can be achieved by control of pests and diseases, without using pesticides or their minimal use, minimal need for water, regulating microclimate, decomposition of waste, and regulation of nutrient cycles and crop pollination etc. Although people have shown that most pollinators including the bees are negatively impacted by various pesticides, there are still large groups of people who say that it is not. But results of meta-analyses that have been done putting together more than 300 to 500 studies of the impact of pesticides on pollinators, there's a large decrease in the number of pollinators in any given locality.

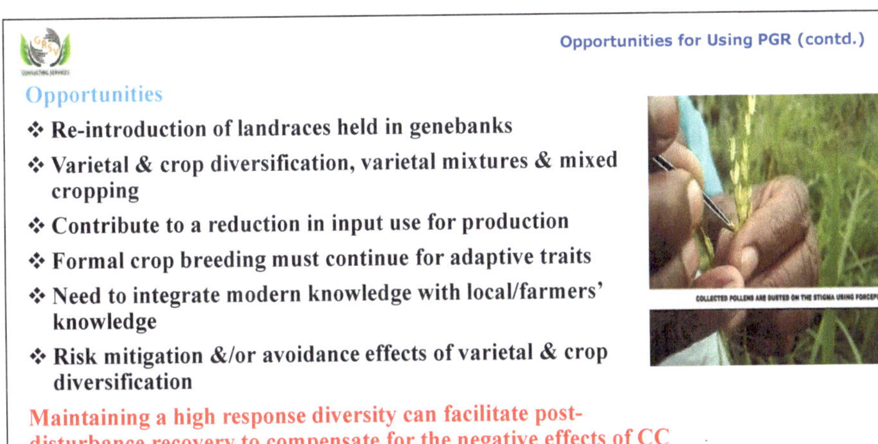

An example of opportunities that are available to us is the reintroduction of landraces held in genebanks on farms. I remember way back when I used to work at ICRISAT, some farmers used to request landraces that they used to grow in their fields which we collected and conserved in the genebank. Unfortunately at that time, the germplasm distribution policy was not very conducive to this, as the general public was not considered as 'bonafide' users. Only the breeders and other researchers anywhere in the world were considered eligible for supply. However, later, this changed and many genebanks around the globe are now doing it and there have been examples of successful reintroductions. Presently, several farmers/growers maintain on their farm out of their interest a significant number of landraces of different or single crops and we refer to them as custodian farmers. Reintroduction or even introduction of farmer-improved varieties will be easier if there is networking of custodian farmers, promoted and supported by either public or NGO organizations.

As noted earlier, most of the material held in genebanks represent clonal materials and single cuttings and bud wood cuttings, and are from single trees. They do not represent the genetic diversity that is required to form a landrace over time. In the current literature, one will see that a considerable amount of work is now looking at crop diversification, varietal mixtures, etc. For example, when we used to collect them from farmer's fields we noticed 18 to 28 different species grown in a small patch of land. Those things have disappeared slowly over the years with monoculture farming taking over. Now there are a few scientists extolling farmers to go back to that system. It may not be a mixture of 18 to 28 genetically diverse entities, but at least a few of them.

Regarding minimizing inputs in agriculture, we may not necessarily go back to what is called either zero farming or zero-input farming or natural farming. However, there is a certain need for rethinking on the quality and quantity of inputs that are being used in agriculture and how to reduce most of the inputs to make agriculture sustainable. It is imperative to keep soil, environmental and human health in mind. Formal crop breeding must continue for adaptive traits. There is a need to integrate modern knowledge with local and farmer knowledge to improve risk mitigation and avoidance effects of varietal and crop diversification. We need a little more effort in actually putting figures on most of it. Even now some other things are coming back based on studies done in labs and institutional fields. There is very little based on farmer's field experimentation. For example, maintaining the high-response diversity can facilitate post-disturbance recovery to compensate for the negative effect of climate change. There will be a definite effect of climate change, but I think we can survive if we start practising this right now rather than later.

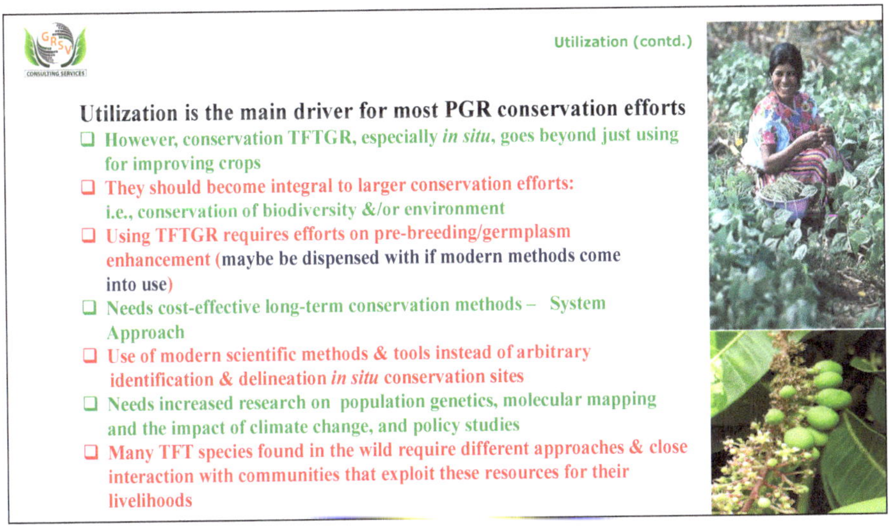

We all know that utilization is the main driver of all our efforts to conserve and manage plant genetic resources. The user may be in the current times or in the future. When we are specifically talking about tropical fruit genetic resources, especially *in situ* conservation, it goes beyond utilizing. It is the survival of humankind itself that will determine how much *in situ* conservation is practised not just for tropical fruit genetic resources but for most of the genetic resources, especially the wild genetic resources. This will have a tremendous bearing on the future. I believe that they should become an integral part of a larger conservation effort. They cannot be done on a piecemeal basis, but they should become part of a larger strategy. In addition, we should stop looking at utilisation keeping pure economic profitability in mind, but for sustaining human and ecosystem health in future. Use should focus on not just economic development, but also on social development and environmental protection. The national utilization strategy requires rethinking several aspects of tropical fruit trees. It requires pre-breeding, genetic enhancements etc., along with the conservation of nature. But if modern methods come into use, maybe some of these need not be carried out at least for some species. Cost-effective long-term conservation methods are required, and this can be achieved if we use a systems approach. The systems approach is a complex concept to understand but once you understand then you will see the logic behind it. It is something like concepts used while project planning and formulation and certain methodology is used for this purpose. The system approach is not just a project planning approach but it is used for the implementation of the project also. While it is already being used in various other production systems, it is just making an entry into agriculture. We published a paper about four years ago on this approach. However, for germplasm management, it is still in the formative stages. The use of modern scientific methods and tools instead of arbitrary identification and delineation of *in situ* conservation sites will require more on-the-ground information, and establish benchmarks for different locations and for species that may be conserved in those locations and then proceed from there. It also needs increased research on population genetics, molecular mapping and the impact of climate change. We need much larger sets of disciplines to deal with genetic resources, especially for use in woody perennial species such as tropical fruit trees. This is one of the reasons why most genetic resource specialists are generalists and need to be able to use methods from diverse disciplines. They have a generic understanding of agriculture, and the systems are not specializing in any one particular aspects that are required for proper genetic resource management.

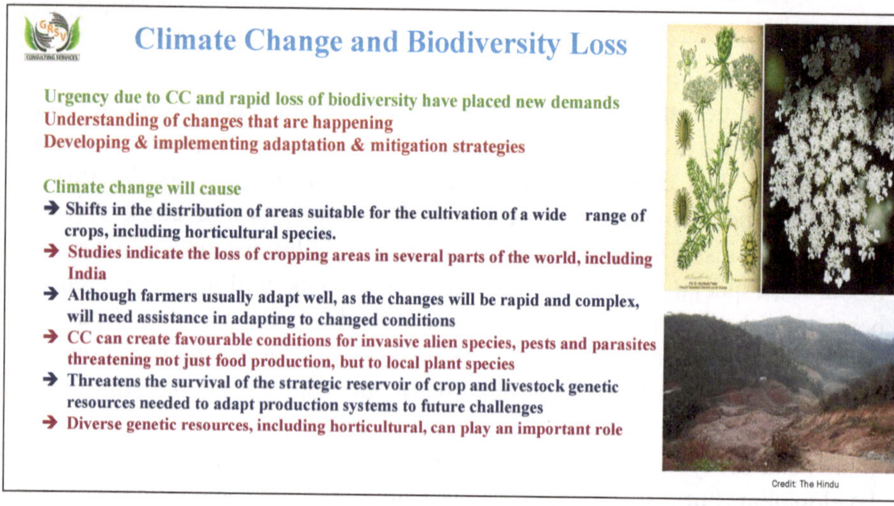

As noted earlier, biodiversity is both a victim of climate change and a tool for mitigating its impact. So, we need to first understand changes that are happening in biodiversity at large and then move on to how we can use it to reduce the negative impact on food production, the environment and ecosystems. Climate change has been shown to cause changes in the distribution of plant species, including tropical fruit species. Using climate data and specific software, predictions on the shift in areas suitable for localization of a wide range of plant species caused by climate change can be made so that areas can be pinpointed for collecting. Similarly, shifts in boundaries of cultivation are expected to occur. This can hurt the yields of certain crops, while some cultivators can take advantage of the shifts and extend cultivation into areas previously thought to be unsuitable. We need to be vigilant as new invasive species can become more virulent and impede agricultural production. It can also affect the existence of genebanks as some areas wherein the present genebanks are maintained can become unsuitable. We need to be prepared with duplicate collections as well as the ability to quickly move the collections into new locations. In all these cases, tropical fruit genetic resources have a role to play.

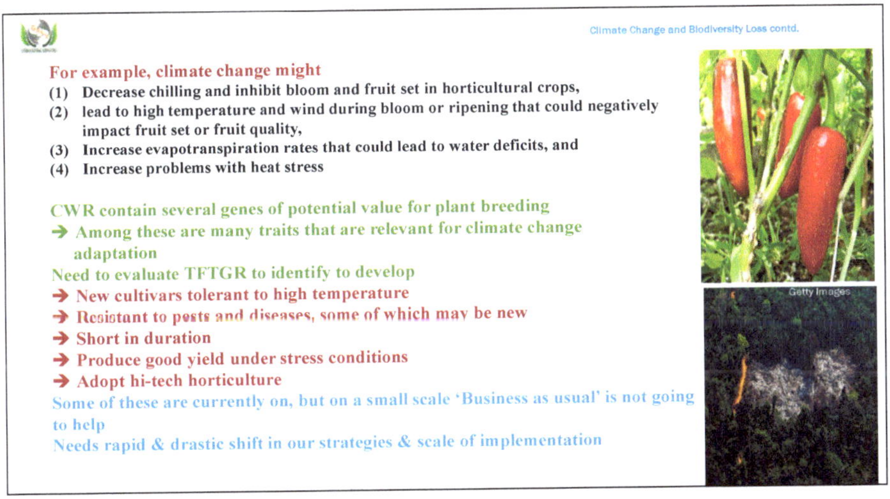

Concerning fruit species specifically, evidence is becoming available on changes induced by climate change in flowering time changes (early or late), time taken to fruit maturity and harvesting seasons. In conditions beyond 35°C, ethylene production is affected thus interfering with maturity processes in many fruit species. Loss in genetic diversity can lead to adaptation issues in future, for example, in grapes for wine production. These shifts not only interfere with fruit production systems but also field genebank management. Such changes are also known 5 to affect fruit quality to a great extent. There are other hosts of effects. Many solutions may be found in genetic resources available to us, but it requires careful evaluation and screening of germplasm and identification and testing of genetic material either for direct use or for inclusion in crop improvement programmes. No doubt in many major fruit species considerable genetic resources have been assembled, but the changing climate makes it imperative to screen through the material, identify material that can be used in changed environments and scale up quickly to cultivation by farmers.

Human Dimension

- **Probably the most important aspect of any conservation effort**
- **Conservation & use depends on felt needs, understanding & attitude of people that are dependent & involved**
- **Do not ignore the needs of farmers & consumers**

Human elements include

People in general

- **Improved understanding that the farming community & consumers of agricultural products need to benefit**
- **All efforts are sustainable should & are amenable to changes that may have to be made as technologies change over time, i.e. not static**

Let us now look at the human dimension in germplasm management, in general, which are applicable to the case of tropical fruit tree genetic resources. I feel that the human dimension aspect has been woefully neglected in genetic resources conservation and utilisation. While conservation and use require different skills and understandings, the attitudes of people towards the entire process are important, for example, they should not be disappointed if they fail to see the fruits of labour soon. Unfortunately, the human dimension aspects do not have specific goals, e.g., reaching a market using a plant-breeding product, etc., the goal in this case may be a moving goalpost. With the impact of climate change, most of the objectives of germplasm management have changed. However, most of the objectives of plant breeding like tolerance to drought, tolerance to diseases, etc., have remained the same, while the objectives of genetic resources conservation and use have changed. This is a simplistic way of describing it for easy understanding. We need, in germplasm management areas, people with a better understanding of the farming community, forest dwellers, tribal/indigenous people and preferences of both growers and consumers. There is a need to balance the interests of farming communities and their economic profit and prices that are acceptable to consumers so that the community benefits as a whole. All efforts need to keep sustainability in focus and there is no exception to that rule in future. They should be able to adapt technologies for better germplasm management as they are developed, making sure that the technologies are cost-effective and sustainable. All this requires human capital that can be adaptive and efficient at the same time.

Human Dimension (contd.)

Scientific & technical

- Need competent scientists & managers
- Need to be in tune with the basic philosophy of conservation for use in the present & future generations
- Not averse to filed work
- Be able to relate to & work closely with farmers & indigenous communities

Policymakers

- Awareness of the role & significance of TFTGR conservation & use in sustainable horticultural conservation, production & reduction of poverty
- Policy support for conservation efforts, along with the requisite funds

Collaboration among all actors

- Networking & collaborating with each other that transcends individual or institutional interests & barriers & even nations
- Multi-disciplinary, multi-institutional and multi-sectoral cooperation (3M approach) PLUS Regional & International collaboration

Let us now look at the scientific and technical skills that people should have to work in this area. For one thing, as noted earlier on, germplasm managers need to be well versed in several aspects of agronomy, biology, and economics, that is being a generalist and not a specialist. Of course, in the end, one could be a plant genetic resources specialist! Recognition of this has come around a bit late and there is also a change in the attitude about training, especially, the youngsters. Now more people are participating in conserving biodiversity, especially at the school and college levels. However, this change is not happening fast enough. The scientific and technical personnel involved in plant genetic resources work need to be competent scientists and they need to be in tune with the basic philosophy of conservation i.e. should have an understanding of the goal of conservation. They should understand that we are not only conserving for the present but also for use in the future by future generations and that use is not just for economic profitability. That means we have to get rid of some of the greed that may be there within us. We are struggling here to keep things the way they have been (i.e. being sustainable), to the extent possible, so that future generations can continue at least at the current levels of what we have been living with. They should not be averse to fieldwork - of course, that is common for agricultural fieldwork. In addition to that, there is an extensive requirement for going into the wild and collecting materials and information. So should be prepared to do that and be able to relate and work closely with farmers and indigenous communities. It requires quite a bit of our participatory and research methods to be used. The working style, therefore, should be cooperative and collaborative.

For sure, one cannot work in isolation. For policymakers, while there is a need for increased awareness, it is not enough if they say that agricultural biodiversity (and biodiversity) is very important and that excellent work in biodiversity conservation is being done by our programmes, etc. They have to facilitate in terms of policy support, in terms of funding support, etc. There is a lot of 'greenwashing' going on around the globe including India. But greenwashing is not going to help to conserve and utilize biodiversity. Policymakers should be able to constitute critical reviews of the work that has been carried out each year and revise the methods and objectives as need be and not continue with business as usual. Usually, policymakers tend to consider any criticism as negativity and go on with the business.

Collaboration among all the actors is the key and without cooperation no genetic resources management is possible. Individual custodian farmers have been collecting and conserving genetic diversity in their fields. However, even they have obtained many of the materials in cooperation with other farmers. This is a great effort and we badly need networking of those people so that they can further collaborate and continue to do the good work. Conservation work cannot be done in isolation. There is an absolute need for genebank managers to be aware of the needs of crop improvement researchers and should collaborate. We need to get rid of the tag that genetic resources conservation work as a service and the personnel should be treated on equal footing. So, what we need is the '3M approach' - A multi-disciplinary, multi-institutional, and multi-structural approach to manage all aspects of genetic diversity.

Concluding Remarks

- Interdependency: No country is self-sufficient
- Need to develop strategies for conservation of HGR - fully support, participate & implement the conventions, treaties & agreements that aim to effectively conserve & sustainably use
- South, SE Asia & South America are rich in TFT wild relatives, however, their economic value, value as genetic resources, a means of livelihood & associated cultural values are seldom demonstrated
- Multidimensional problems: Resolution of problems surrounding conservation & use of TFTGR requires the attention of all stakeholders
- Issues that need to be addressed are:
  - Collecting & Exploration
  - *In situ*/on-farm conservation
  - Evaluation and & utilization
  - Change in the mindset of people involved

➔ Above all, sustainability needs to be central to all endeavours

To conclude in short, we know that no country is self-sufficient in plant genetic resources which it requires to meet its needs. As one can see this fact by looking at the introduction of many species over centuries. For example, we in India depend to a large extent on introduced plant species. Look at how dragon fruit (*Hylocereus undatus*), a lowly cactus out of Central America, initially cultivated in the backyards of Vietnam is becoming a major commercial success in India. However, now with biodiversity and plant genetic resources being a national heritage, the exchange of genetic material of any kind has become very difficult. Even within the region and with the changes to the biodiversity conservation and Biodiversity Acts, I am pretty doubtful about where we will be going in the future in this area. We need to develop strategies for conservation of genetic resources including horticultural genetic resources. We may have to make do with what is available to us with little expectation of obtaining these resources from another country or region. We need to fully support, participate and implement various conventions, treaties and demands. South and Southeast Asia, and South America are very rich in tropical fruit trees and their wild relatives, which require special attention. Their value may not be realized now but will be realized in future as the climate tends to change, new actors come into play, and new species take over some of the areas. Maybe in future, better-quality products may be there. We face multi-dimensional problems and hence require a lot of effort, especially in convincing and getting the stakeholders to act in a scientifically sound manner and that is important. Issues that need to be addressed, in future, mainly are collecting exploration *in situ*, on-farm evaluation, utilization and change in the mindset of people. Sustainability should be the driving force. Everything we do has to be sustainable and the sustainable development process should be augmented with whatever we do.

Questions & Answers

(Q) Vybhav Bansod: How can we use underutilized fruit crops in fruit production?

(A) V Ramanatha Rao: I think the answer is in the question itself. If we have an underutilized fruit species, first, it needs to be brought under cultivation. Then we evaluate and compare it with other fruits that are already available in the market. We need to establish whether these fruits will be liked by people and whether they would pay money to buy them. Within the forested areas, forest people and fringe dwellers would always use these species. But to bring it out as a marketable product one has to follow the steps of what people did in the domestication process. First, bring it under cultivation, check to know what kind of yields they produce and check the consumer preferences. Only then, one can go forward.

(Q) Mahesh Kulkarni: While lot of research work is going on in biotech area, bioinformatics and genomic aspects of tropical fruits. Many research paper is available. However, why is it that no single variety has been released by any institution so far by using this information?

(A) V Ramanatha Rao: This question is better answered by people who are involved in this area. But my simplistic answer is that, for example in India, the policies governing the environmental release of genetically modified organisms (GMOs) are not clear which applies to all crops. However, as I showed in one of my slides, GMOs in papaya and tomato, have been produced. Even in some fruits, they are available in the market in other countries which have a favourable policy for releasing them.

(Q) Ramalinga Reddy This was a nice and exhaustive presentation. There are certain difficulties when one is handling germplasm of especially tropical fruit species. My comment is that in this process they should be classified whether it is a high-risk species or medium risk species or low-risk species. Depending on their risk category, they would require certain kinds of infrastructure facilities for the conservation as well as evaluation. Risk assessment should be based on viruses, viroids and phytoplasmas which are hosted by these fruit tree species. It is necessary to integrate testing procedures for these complex organisms in germplasm explorations and conservation procedures, whether in situ conservation or ex-situ conservation. Another comment is about the germplasm of tropical horticultural crops. This is one of the weakest areas where not much exploitation is done. There are a lot of wild species which can be used for cultivation purposes and some of them also may be near extinction.

(A) V Ramanatha Rao: I didn't go into the details of this issue as it is part of the challenges that tropical fruit tree genetic resources have. For any perennial plant species conservation, it is very important to see that it is as much free from any disease especially viruses as you mentioned. This is one of the reasons why in many of the fruit and vegetable species, *in-vitro* conservation has been adopted. Also, we should not be using terms like high risk or low risk, because, for most of the plant people, it would mean in terms of the existence of the species and whether they would go extinct sooner or later. I am fully in agreement with you regarding the importance of managing disease-free germplasm material, whether with symptoms or symptomless.

(Q) **Sudhakar Reddy:** I have 15 years of horticulture experience. I notice that the fundamentals are not being followed in their simplest terms before we can even talk of the conservation of germplasm of tropical fruit trees. I have seen Botanical Gardens in London and Malaysia. One is managed in the highest form and the other in a simple form. There they have been maintaining using in-situ methods using marigolds as a trap crop as pollinisers and the pollinators are helping plants being raised there. Also, I think it is important to correlate the microbiome of the soil with the material grown. The fundamentals are known, and the principles are known. Microbiomes should be given importance, especially by using the proper biofertilizers.

(A) **V Ramanatha Rao:** This is part of what we call how you deal with the agronomical aspects of field gene banks management. Even way back in 2002, we prepared a training guide for building genebanks. They have looked into these practices. Many gene banks do not have the resources to follow them strictly. As you rightly said, science is available but the practice is not good enough because of a lack of resources of many kinds. I mentioned human resources, among different important resources. It is a question of how much we can put in and how much we can get out. Agronomic practices are not going to change the basic genetic constitution of the plant which we are trying to grow. We are not bothered about the yield aspect here. We are bothered about the continued existence of the tree. There are various thresholds to be set in and trade-offs to be made.

(Q) **Suren Tikoo:** You mentioned that utilization of the variability in breeding is the least. I wanted to add that it is the least even in the crops where we have done a lot of interspecific breeding. In the top five crops including crops like tomato, studies show that we have not even utilized five per cent of the available variability, and, in fruit crops probably even less of that variability has gone into breeding. I think that there is a need for a policy-level decision on how to support that kind of breeding. I also don't think that enough attention is given to germplasm conservation. On the human level, I think botany students need to have a course on food crop taxonomy, etc. so that skilled people are available to get into the germplasm jobs. Thank you for an excellent lecture. It has made me think about lots of other things.

(A) **V Ramanatha Rao:** I would like to thank Dr Tikoo for the support. I also would like to point out that the utilization is not even five per cent. The actual estimates of utilization indicate less than one per cent. In fruit crops even less.

